D0553303

D.
05/15 SEATON VALLEY LIBRARY
This book is due for return on or before the last date shown below.

2 5 AUG 2015

1 3 NOV 2015

© 2006 Alligator Books Limited

Author: Prof. Michael Benton BSc, PhD
Illustrator: John Sibbick

Published by Alligator Books Limited
Gadd House, Arcadia Avenue
London N3 2JU

All rights reserved. No part of this book may be reproduced or utilized in any form or by any means, electronic or
mechanical, including photocopying, recording or by any information storage and retrieval system, without permission
in writing from the publisher except by a reviewer who may quote brief passages in a review.

Printed in China

CONTENTS

FEARSOME MINI-BEASTS

Not all dinosaurs were huge. Some of the smallest, fastest and fiercest dinosaurs were smaller than you are.

The first dinosaurs were tiny. The smallest baby dinosaur was *Mussaurus*, a tiny prosauropod from the Late Triassic Period. *Mussaurus* was about the size of a kitten, measuring only 20 centimetres long. The smallest adult dinosaur was the meat-eating *Compsognathus* from the Late Jurassic Period. It measured about 70 centimetres long – about the same as a medium-sized dog, although it weighed much less.

Small reptiles often lived alongside the biggest dinosaurs ever to have roamed Earth, such as the 22-metre-long *Brachiosaurus*. Small dinosaurs like *Compsognathus* survived because they were skillful predators. Others were successful because they had well-developed defence systems and could outrun, and possibly outwit, the larger beasts of their day.

Theropods

Some of the scariest dinosaurs were small meat-eating theropods. Vulture-like ornithomimids were light, fast-moving hunters. Their strong hands had either fingers or claws. They used their hands to grasp and hold down wriggling prey.

Struthiomimus

Oviraptor

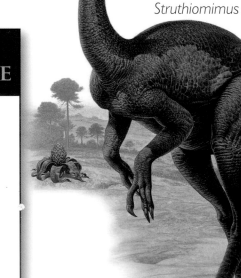

FACTFILE: THE DINOSAUR AGE

- The Mesozoic Era lasted from 250 to 65 million years ago. Mesozoic means 'middle life'.

- The Cretaceous Period lasted from 150 to 65 million years ago. Cretaceous comes from the Latin *creta* ('chalk').

- The Jurassic Period lasted from 205 to 150 million years ago. It was named after the Jura Mountains, France.

- The Triassic Period lasted from 250 to 205 million years ago. Triassic means 'three-part'.

Prosauropods
Dog-sized Anchisaurus was one of the first vegetarian dinosaurs. It had a long, strong and whip-like tail to defend itself from predators.

Anchisaurus

Tenontosaurus

Dryosaurus

Ornithopods
Like many plant-eating ornithopods, bird-like hypsilophodontids had powerful legs and strong, balancing tails to help them run swiftly.

Hypsilophodon

Dromiceiomimus

Ceratopsians
As a bipedal dinosaur with a parrot-shaped beak and stong, grasping hands, Psittacosaurus could feed from trees as well as low-lying plants. Early ceratopsians were human-sized.

Psittacosaurus

HOW DO I SAY THAT?

● **MESOZOIC**
MESS-OH-ZOH-IK

● **CRETACEOUS**
KRET-AY-SHUSS

● **JURASSIC**
JOO-RASS-IK

● **TRIASSIC**
TRY-ASS-IK

5

LIVING DINOSAURS

UP CLOSE

Some small dinosaurs have skeletons almost identical to *Archaeopteryx* – the oldest known bird. *Archaeopteryx* was one of the most famous fossil finds. It showed that dinosaur ancestors of birds must have developed the ability to fly. *Archaeopteryx* fossils date from the Late Jurassic Period and were found in Germany. The fossils clearly show the skeleton and delicate outlines of the feathers, which were preserved as soft imprints in the ancient mud.

When the first *Archaeopteryx* fossil was found in 1861, it provided the 'missing link' in the story of evolution between reptiles and birds. Paleontologists had always thought that birds evolved from reptiles. They pointed to clues such as the scales on a bird's legs. But the *Archaeopteryx* discovery provided much stronger evidence. *Archaeopteryx* was a bird with feathers and wings, but it also had some dinosaur features, such as teeth, claws and a long, bony tail. In fact, the skeleton of *Archaeopteryx* is remarkably similar to the little theropod – *Compsognathus*.

Archaeopteryx *fossil*
The first bird had wings that were identical in structure to the wings of a modern bird. The first bird had long, finger-like feathers. The wing muscles would not have been as strong as a modern bird, but the flying action was probably the same.

Archaeopteryx

Compsognathus

Skull comparison
The teeth and eye sockets in an Archaeopteryx skull are reptilian features and are similar to those of the dinosaur Compsognathus.

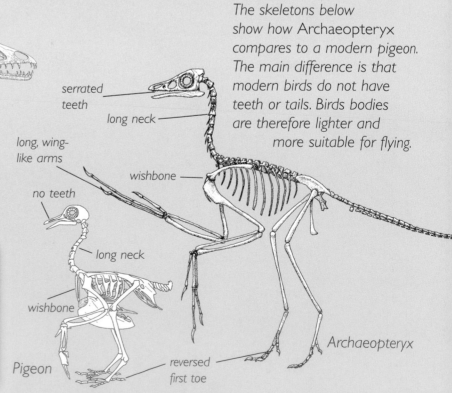

serrated teeth

long neck

long, wing-like arms

no teeth

long neck

wishbone

Pigeon

reversed first toe

wishbone

Archaeopteryx

Dinosaurs and birds
The skeletons below show how Archaeopteryx compares to a modern pigeon. The main difference is that modern birds do not have teeth or tails. Birds bodies are therefore lighter and more suitable for flying.

DINO DICTIONARY

- **Paleontologist:** a scientist who studies fossils
- **Evolution:** the development of animals over a very long time

Early bird

In life, Archaeopteryx would have looked like a bird. But it had not evolved with many of the weight-saving devices of modern birds, such as the beak and the stumpy tail.

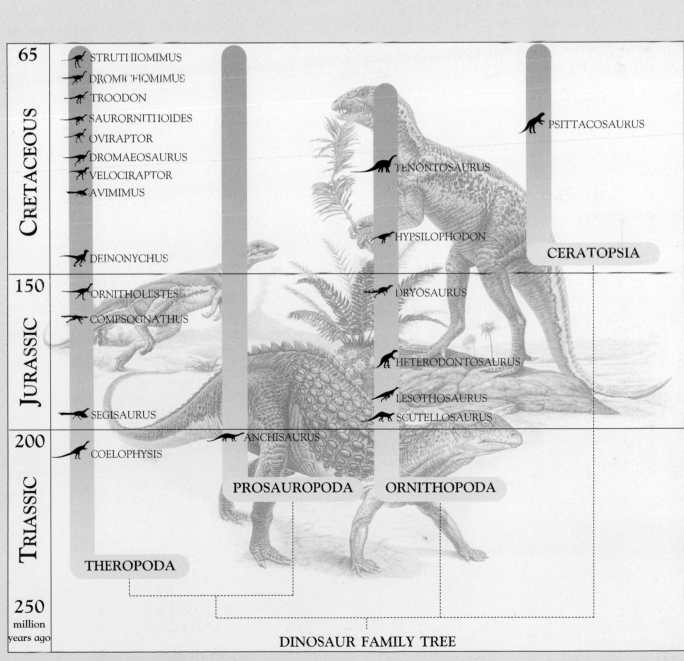

65		
	STRUTHIOMIMUS	
	DROMICEIOMIMUS	
	TROODON	
	SAURORNITHOIDES	
	OVIRAPTOR	
	DROMAEOSAURUS	PSITTACOSAURUS
	VELOCIRAPTOR	TENONTOSAURUS
	AVIMIMUS	
		HYPSILOPHODON
	DEINONYCHUS	
		CERATOPSIA
150	ORNITHOLESTES	DRYOSAURUS
	COMPSOGNATHUS	
		HETERODONTOSAURUS
		LESOTHOSAURUS
	SEGISAURUS	SCUTELLOSAURUS
200	COELOPHYSIS ANCHISAURUS	
	PROSAUROPODA	**ORNITHOPODA**
	THEROPODA	
250 million years ago		

CRETACEOUS

JURASSIC

TRIASSIC

DINOSAUR FAMILY TREE

PATTERNS & FEATHERS

Small dinosaurs may have been just as successful at hunting prey as large dinosaurs.

It is difficult to know how dinosaurs looked because fossils cannot tell us about the colour of their skin. Many reptiles today, such as lizards and snakes, have colourful skin patterns. Some dinosaurs might have been the same. Colourful skin patterns would have helped to ward off bigger predators. *Segisaurus* – a small theropod and a relative of *Coelophysis* – is shown here with colourful body stripes. Another curious theropod was *Avimimus*. Its skeleton interested scientists because of its mixture of bird-like and dinosaur features. The fossil of *Avimimus* showed that the dinosaur had a ridge along the arm bones. Birds have a similar structure to fix their feathers in place. As a result, scientists believe that many dinosaurs were feathered.

Segisaurus
This little hunter had short arms and three fingers on each hand. It had long, powerful legs, so it may have been a fast-mover.

HOW DO I SAY THAT?

● **AVIMIMUS**
AH-VIH-MIME-US
● **SEGISAURUS**
SEG-IH-SAW-RUS

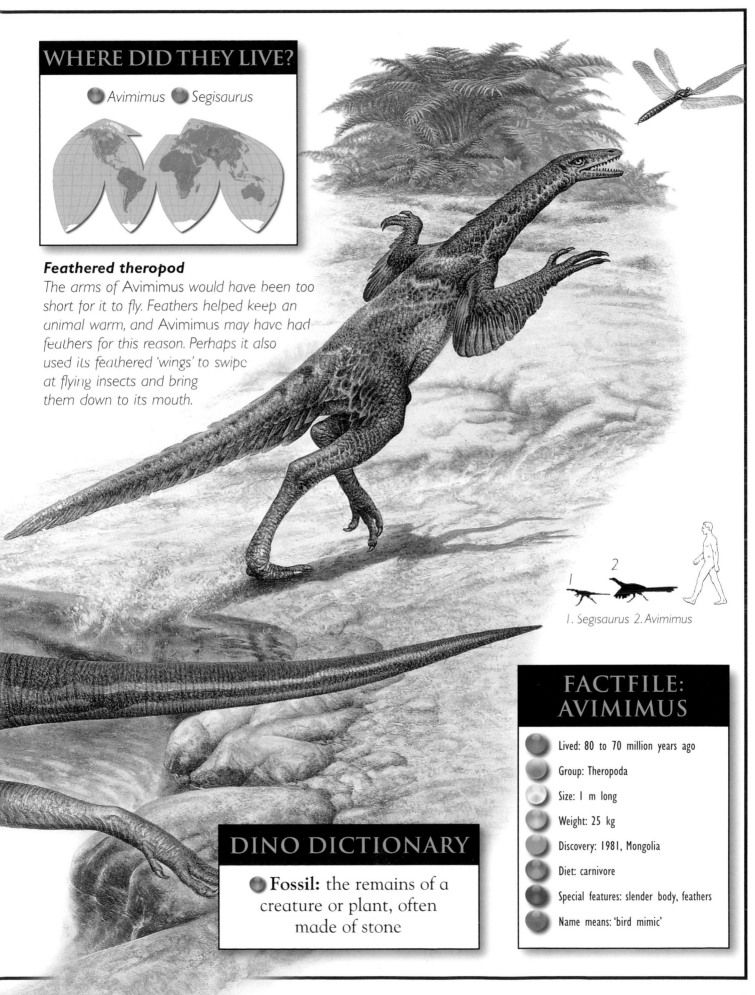

Feathered theropod

The arms of Avimimus would have been too short for it to fly. Feathers helped keep an animal warm, and Avimimus may have had feathers for this reason. Perhaps it also used its feathered 'wings' to swipe at flying insects and bring them down to its mouth.

1. Segisaurus 2. Avimimus

FACTFILE: AVIMIMUS

● Lived: 80 to 70 million years ago

● Group: Theropoda

● Size: 1 m long

● Weight: 25 kg

● Discovery: 1981, Mongolia

● Diet: carnivore

● Special features: slender body, feathers

● Name means: 'bird mimic'

DINO DICTIONARY

● **Fossil:** the remains of a creature or plant, often made of stone

MEAT-EATERS

Tryannosaurus rex was a fearsome predator, but small predatory theropods were just as fierce.

The first dinosaurs were small, fast-running, meat-eating theropods. Theropods ('beast feet') walked on two back legs and had sharp claws on their hands and bird-like feet. They used their hands to grab their prey and possibly to carry away pieces of meat to devour later.

Coelphysis was one of the earliest theropods. _Ornitholestes_ and _Compsognathus_ came later in the Late Jurassic Period. All three reptiles had similar features and habits. They had slender bodies, long flexible necks, powerful legs, sharp teeth and strong clawed hands. Groups of _Coelphysis_ fossils were found in North America. This suggests that these agile dinosaurs may have hunted in packs, like wild wolves today. Since the fossils were found in a group, these dinosaurs may have died together in a drought.

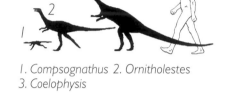

1. Compsognathus 2. Ornitholestes
3. Coelophysis

HOW DO I SAY THAT?

● **COELOPHYSIS**
SEEL-OH-FY-SIS

● **COMPSOGNATHUS**
KOMP-SOG-NAY-THUS

● **ORNITHOLESTES**
OR-NITH-OH-LESS-TEEZ

Sharp-toothed hunter
Ornitholestes _had sharp teeth that pointed inwards, trapping prey in its mouth. This dinosaur may have snatched flesh from prey that had been killed by larger dinosaurs._

FACTFILE: COELOPHYSIS

- Lived: 230 to 220 million years ago
- Group: Theropoda
- Size: 3 m long, 1.5 m tall
- Weight: 45 kg
- Discovery: 1881, New Mexico, USA
- Diet: carnivore
- Special features: slender body, long tail
- Name means: 'hollow form'

Slim and ferocious
Coelophysis was a small but merciless predator. A skeleton of a younger dinosaur was found in the stomach of an adult.

Small and speedy
Compsognathus was one of the smallest dinosaurs. It was about as big as a cat. Compsognathus was an active predator, chasing small prey such as lizards and insects. Its two-fingered hands were unusual for dinosaurs of the time.

WHERE DID THEY LIVE?

- Coelophysis and Ornitholestes
- Compsognathus

THE OSTRICH DINOSAURS

Ornithomimids were fast-running, meat-eating hunters but, strangely, they had no teeth.

Why didn't the ornithomimids have any teeth? They may have eaten food, such as insects and eggs, for which teeth were not needed. It is also likely that the ornithomimids had sharp-edged beaks, like modern eagles and vultures. These beaks were used to kill prey by tearing up the flesh.

Struthiomimus

With its speedy legs and strong hands, Struthiomimus *may have hunted insects, such as dragonflies.* Struthiomimus *was probably too big an animal to survive on just insects, however. It is likely it also hunted lizards and other small animals.*

Coming to get you!
Ostrich dinosaurs had long, strong fingers with claws to grab small animals and tear them apart.

HOW DO I SAY THAT?

- **DROMICEIOMIMUS**
  DROM-IK-AY-OH-MIME-US
- **OVIRAPTOR**
  OVE-IH-RAP-TOR
- **STRUTHIOMIMUS**
  STROOTH-EE-OH-MIME-US

1. Oviraptor
2. Struthiomimus
3. Dromiceiomimus

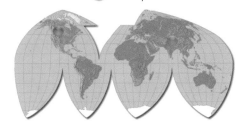

Dromiceiomimus and Struthiomimus

Oviraptor

Strange head

Oviraptor had an unusual skull with a horn-like structure over its snout. The purpose of this nose horn is not known.

Dromiceiomimus

This dinosaur was a close relative of Struthiomimus but it had a shorter back and more slender legs. When Dromiceiomimus chased its prey, it tucked up its arms and stuck its tail out stiffly to act as a counterbalance.

Run like a horse

Ornithomimids appeared in the Late Cretaceous Period. They had long, slender back legs like modern ostriches. They may have run at speeds of 50 kilometres per hour – as fast as a race horse.

Egg thief?

Although Oviraptor was not a true ornithomimid, it was feathered just like an bird. Oviraptor ('egg thief') was named when the first fossils were found near nests in Mongolia. Recent studies have shown that these nests actually belonged to Oviraptor. The dinosaur was looking after its own eggs, not stealing them!

FACTFILE: STRUTHIOMIMUS

Lived: 75 to 65 million years ago

Group: Theropoda

Size: 3 to 4 m long

Weight: 100 kg

Discovery: 1917, Alberta, Canada

Diet: carnivore

Special features: long powerful legs, toothless jaws

Name means: 'ostrich mimic'

BIG-EYED & BRAINY

Dinosaurs had very small brains in relation to the size of their bodies. However, the troodontids were amongst the dinosaurs with the largest brains.

Troodontids like *Saurornithoides* and *Troodon* were fast-moving, lightly built theropods. Their bodies were similar to the ornithomimids. They had ostrich-like necks, small heads, long legs and tails. But troodontids had stronger hands and feet, with huge slashing claws.

For their body size, troodontids had brains that were bigger than the normal size for dinosaurs. This could mean they may have been the most intelligent! By filling a fossil skull with dry lentils, then tipping them into a measuring jug, scientists have worked out the size of many dinosaur's brains.

WHERE DID THEY LIVE?

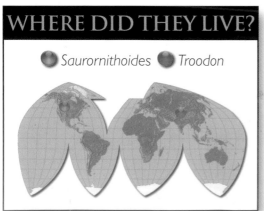

● *Saurornithoides* ● *Troodon*

Knife-like claws

Saurornithoides used the claws on its feet to kill its prey. It grabbed small mammals and lizards and held them tight while tearing the flesh with its teeth. This dinosaur had to rely on its hands and feet, because its teeth were quite small and could not have been used to kill its prey.

FACTFILE: SAURORNITHOIDES

- Lived: 85 to 70 million years ago
- Group: Theropoda
- Size: 2 m long
- Weight: 50 kg
- Discovery: 1923, Mongolia
- Diet: carnivore
- Special features: big brain, beady eyes
- Name means: 'bird-like reptile'

1. Troodon   2. Saurornithoides

Big, beady eyes

Troodon had big, beady eyes set high up on the snout so it could look forwards as well as sideways. Most dinosaurs had their eyes set on the side of their heads like a horse, so each eye saw a different scene. Troodontids may have been able to see in three dimensions like we can.

HOW DO I SAY THAT?

- **SAURORNITHOIDES**
  SAWR-OR-NITH-OIDE-EEZ
- **TROODON**
  TROO-DON

THE SLASHERS

The dromaeosaurids may have been human-sized dinosaurs but their sickle-shaped claw on the second toe of each foot made them ferocious monsters.

The first dromaeosaurid fossils were found about 100 years ago, but scientists could not tell what these dinosaurs looked like because the fossils were incomplete. Then, in 1964, full skeletons of *Deinonychus* were found in North America. *Deinonychus* had good eyesight and a large head so it probably had a relatively big brain for a dinosaur. It had long legs and arms and a stiff tail for balance, so it may have been a fast runner. *Velociraptor* can be distinguished from *Deinonychus* and *Dromaeosaurus* by its low, narrow head. The differences in head shape may reflect differences in the diets of these dinosaurs.

However, the most interesting feature of a dromaeosaurid was its huge slashing claws. When attacking prey, *Deinonychus* balanced on one foot, raised its other leg and flicked the claw – tearing a great gash down the side of its victim. This enabled small predators like *Deinonychus* to attack much larger plant-eating dinosaurs.

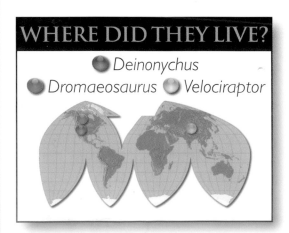

WHERE DID THEY LIVE?

● *Deinonychus*
● *Dromaeosaurus* ○ *Velociraptor*

Dromaeosaurus
Little is known about Dromaeosaurus, the first dromaeosaurid. Only parts of the skull and a few leg bones were found in 1914. Scientists put the rest of the skeleton together when complete fossils of Deinonychus were found.

Big mouth

The jaws of Deinonychus were lined with many backward-pointing teeth. Prey could not escape once it was in the dinosaur's teeth. If it struggled, the animal just moved further down the dinosaur's throat.

FACTFILE: DEINONYCHUS

Lived: 110 to 100 million years ago

Group: Theropoda

Size: 3 m long, 1.5 m tall

Weight: 75 kg

Discovery: 1964, Montana, USA

Diet: carnivore

Special features: slashing claw, stiff tail

Name means: 'terrible claw'

Caught in the act

Velociraptor was an extremely efficient predator better than many larger predators. A fossil from Mongolia shows a Velociraptor locked in a fight with a horned dinosaur called Protoceratops. Velociraptor is shown grasping the head shield of Protoceratops. This suggests that these dinosaurs probably died together in a freak sandstorm. The remains of Velociraptor were not found with Dromaeosaurus and Deinonychus. It is unlikely that they all lived together as shown in this picture.

1. Dromaeosaurus
2. Velociraptor
3. Deinonychus

HOW DO I SAY THAT?

DEINONYCHUS
DINE-ON-IKE-US

DROMAEOSAURUS
DROM-AY-OH-SAW-RUS

VELOCIRAPTOR
VEL-OSS-IH-RAP-TOR

UP CLOSE

SMALL THEROPODS

Every part of the skeleton of a small theropod was designed for quick movement and effective hunting. The skull was narrow and the jaws were powerful. The neck was long and flexible to enable the dinosaur to thrust and dive its head like a snake. The hands were strong, so predators could wrestle their prey to the ground. The legs were long, agile and powerful and designed for running. The whip-like tail provided balance as these pedators pursued their fast-moving prey.

Light headed
Like Compsognauthus, Coelophysis *had a hollow skull and long jaws lined with serrated teeth.*

Compsognathus

The first theropods
Coelophysis *was one of the earliest theropods. It had many features that were similar to other small theropods. It had long arms and relatively short legs, so it could rest on all-fours when feeding.*

Coelophysis

Strong hands
Coelophysis *had fingers on each hand, so it could grasp its prey effectively.*

Nimble predator
Compsognathus *was one of the smallest dinosaurs that ever lived. It had a slender, pointed snout so it could dig deep inside the animal carcass to strip of the meat.*

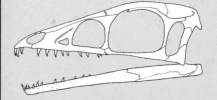

Compsognathus *skull*
This hollow skull was typical of a predator that caught small, fast-moving animals such as lizards and insects.

Clawed hands
Long fingered hands were better at grasping prey, so it is unusual for a small predator like Compsognathus *to have short hands with claws.*

Running legs
Compsognathus *had long, slender legs typical of small, fast-moving dinosaurs. This dinosaur had three long, forward-pointing toes on each foot as well as a backward-pointing fourth toe.*

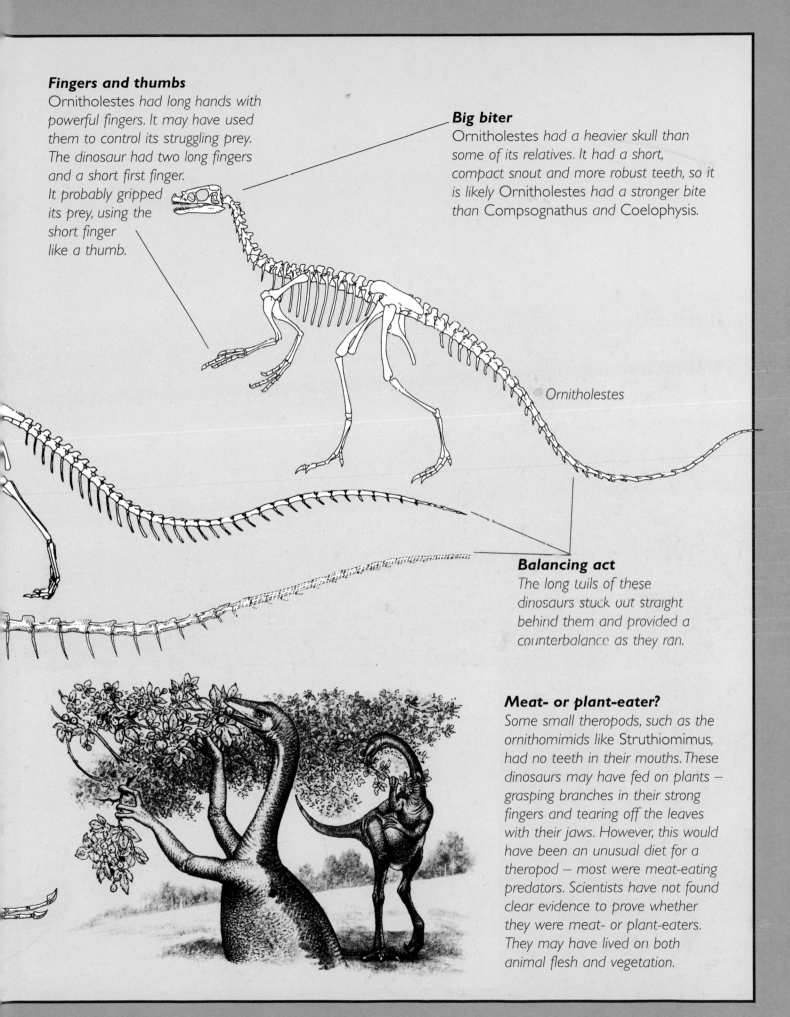

Fingers and thumbs

Ornitholestes *had long hands with powerful fingers. It may have used them to control its struggling prey. The dinosaur had two long fingers and a short first finger. It probably gripped its prey, using the short finger like a thumb.*

Big biter

Ornitholestes *had a heavier skull than some of its relatives. It had a short, compact snout and more robust teeth, so it is likely* Ornitholestes *had a stronger bite than* Compsognathus *and* Coelophysis.

Ornitholestes

Balancing act

The long tails of these dinosaurs stuck out straight behind them and provided a counterbalance as they ran.

Meat- or plant-eater?

Some small theropods, such as the ornithomimids like Struthiomimus, had no teeth in their mouths. These dinosaurs may have fed on plants — grasping branches in their strong fingers and tearing off the leaves with their jaws. However, this would have been an unusual diet for a theropod — most were meat-eating predators. Scientists have not found clear evidence to prove whether they were meat- or plant-eaters. They may have lived on both animal flesh and vegetation.

19

Claw movement when attacking

Claw position when running

UP CLOSE ANATOMY OF A KILLER

Deinonychus was a perfect hunter. Every part of its body – from the tip of its snout to the end of its tail – was designed for speed and ferocity. But the dinosaur's key weapon was the slashing claw on each foot. This required more skill than that shown by any other dinosaur. *Deinonychus* may been good at keeping balance and probably had excellent eyesight as well. It could stand on one leg, slash its victim with the other claw, land back on both feet and twist around ready to strike again.

Vicious weapon

Instead of using its teeth like a typical predator, Deinonychus' main weapons were its legs and its huge claws. When Deinonychus ran, it held its slashing foot upright. However, it could swing its foot through more than 180 degrees to attack its prey.

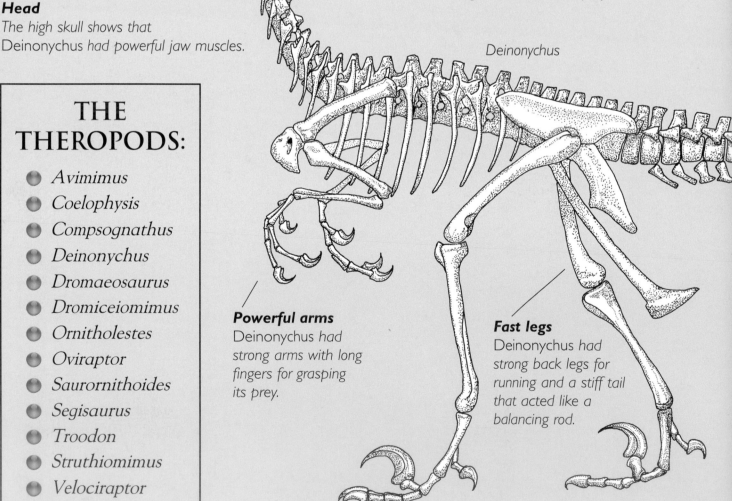

Deinonychus

Head
The high skull shows that Deinonychus *had powerful jaw muscles.*

THE THEROPODS:

- *Avimimus*
- *Coelophysis*
- *Compsognathus*
- *Deinonychus*
- *Dromaeosaurus*
- *Dromiceiomimus*
- *Ornitholestes*
- *Oviraptor*
- *Saurornithoides*
- *Segisaurus*
- *Troodon*
- *Struthiomimus*
- *Velociraptor*

Powerful arms
Deinonychus *had strong arms with long fingers for grasping its prey.*

Fast legs
Deinonychus *had strong back legs for running and a stiff tail that acted like a balancing rod.*

Hunting

It is likely that Deinonychus *hunted large prey in a pack and smaller prey on its own (right). A fossil skeleton of Tenontosaurus — a dinosaur ten times bigger than Deinonychus — was discovered surrounded by several Deinonychus. So five or six Deinonychus may have attacked a larger animal (as shown below) like a pack of wild dogs do today.*

1. Deinonychus *runs up fast from behind as it hunts a smaller dinosaur.*

Flexible and rigid

Deinonychus *had a short, strong back. This allowed it to twist and turn effectively when hunting. Its tail consisted of fine bony rods that made it stiff.*

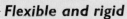

2. Deinonychus *leaps on the back of its prey and sinks its teeth into the soft neck muscles.*

3. *The killing claw rips the victim's belly open, and* Deinonychus *begins its feast.*

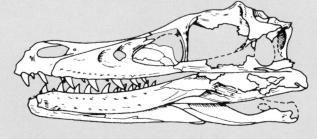

Similar relative

Velociraptor *was a relative of* Deinonychus, *but it had a much flatter skull. Despite the differences in their skulls, the skeletons of the two dinosaurs are very similar, although* Velociraptor *was half the size of* Deinonychus. *This fossilised skull is slightly crushed — you can see how some of the bones do not fit precisely.*

DINO DICTIONARY

Prey: an animal that is hunted

Predator: a flesh-eating animal

Carcass: the dead body of an animal

Skull: the bones of the head

AMAZING ANCHISAURUS

Among the first small plant-eating dinosaurs to appear on Earth were the prosauropods from the Late Triassic Period.

The first prosauropods were small reptiles, even though their later relatives – sauropods like *Apatosaurus* and *Diplodocus* – were giants. One of the smallest prosauropods was *Anchisaurus*. It was the height of a terrier dog but much longer. Fossils of *Anchisaurus* were actually the first dinosaur remains to be found in North America. *Anchisaurus* was lightly built and agile enough to escape quickly from the predatory dinosaurs of its day.

Head and hands
Anchisaurus had a small head and a long neck. Its teeth were small and pencil-shaped, so it probably fed on leaves from bushes and small trees. Anchisaurus *had five fingers on each foot and its broad thumb was armed with a large claw that was used to grasp plants.*

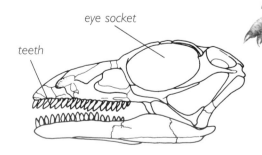

teeth

eye socket

Skull
Anchisaurus had a very large eye socket. Its teeth were coarsely serrated and packed tightly together for grinding up tough plants.

HOW DO I SAY THAT?

●ANCHISAURUS
AN-KIH-SAW-RUS

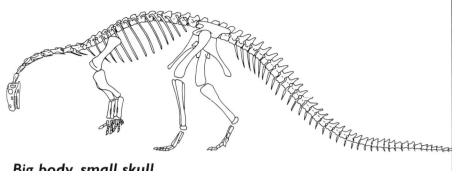

Big body, small skull

Anchisaurus *had a large barrel-shaped body in relation to the size of its tiny skull. This is similar to most plant-eating dinosaurs. Plant-eaters need a bigger stomach to digest raw plant food than meat-eating animals.*

FACTFILE: ANCHISAURUS

Lived: 220 to 200 million years ago

Group: Prosauropoda

Size: 2.5 m long

Weight: 40 kg

Discovery: 1818, Connecticut, USA

Diet: herbivore

Special features: long neck, strong thumb claw

Name means: 'close reptile'

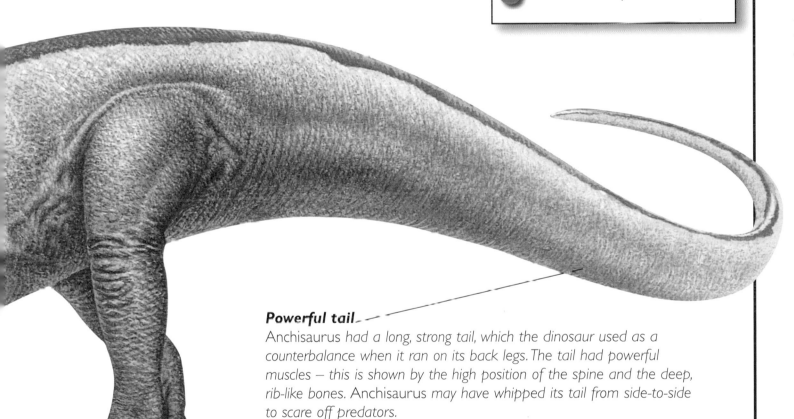

Powerful tail

Anchisaurus *had a long, strong tail, which the dinosaur used as a counterbalance when it ran on its back legs. The tail had powerful muscles — this is shown by the high position of the spine and the deep, rib-like bones.* Anchisaurus *may have whipped its tail from side-to-side to scare off predators.*

Versatile mover

Powerful legs and strong arms enabled Anchisaurus *to walk on all-fours. To break into a run, the dinosaur would only have used its back legs.*

Anchisaurus

WHERE DID THEY LIVE?

Anchisaurus

DINOSAUR DEFENCES

The main group of small, plant-eating dinosaurs were the ornithopods. Some had unusual armour and eating habits.

The first ornithopods lived during the Late Triassic Period. They were small, fast-moving, two-legged animals. The earliest ornithopod was *Lesothosaurus*, which was about the size of a cat. It could dart quickly to escape predators. Its head was primitive and lizard-like compared to later ornithopods. Its larger relative, *Scutellosaurus*, had rows of armour plates along its body. These were set into the skin like the bony scales of a crocodile.

   Heterodontosaurus was similar to *Lesothosaurus,* but it had larger feet and various-sized teeth. It fed differently to *Lesothosaurus.* Instead of just swallowing food, *Heterodontosaurus* chewed everything in its cheek. The long fangs at the sides of the dinosaur's mouth may have used to dig up plant roots from the ground.

HOW DO I SAY THAT?

- **HETERODONTOSAURUS**
  HET-ER-OH-DON'T-OH-SAW-RUS
- **LESOTHOSAURUS**
  LESS-OH-TOE-SAW-RUS
- **SCUTELLOSAURUS**
  SCOOT-ELL-OH-SAW-RUS

Lesothosaurus
This dinosaur was one of the smallest plant-eaters. It used its small, powerful arms to gather up leaves and other plant food to stuff into its mouth. It had lots of sharp, evenly spaced teeth and slender jaws.

Heterodontosaurus

A plant-eating dinosaur whose name means 'mixed-tooth reptile'. Unlike most dinosaurs, Heterodontosaurus had three kinds of teeth: sharp cutting teeth at the front of the jaw, fangs just behind these and grinding teeth in its cheek. It may have fed on tough ferns.

FACTFILE: LESOTHOSAURUS

- Lived: 200 to 190 million years ago
- Group: Ornithopoda
- Size: 90 cm long
- Weight: 10 kg
- Discovery: 1964, Lesotho, southern Africa
- Diet: herbivore
- Special features: small size, strong legs
- Name means: 'Lesotho reptile'

1. Lesothosaurus
2. Heterodontosaurus 3. Scuttellosaurus

Scutellosaurus

With longer arms than Lesothosaurus, this dinosaur may have walked on all-fours. It had an extremely long tail and regular, oval-shaped armour plates all over its body.

WHERE DID THEY LIVE?

Heterodontosaurus and Lesothosaurus

Scutellosaurus

25

SPEEDY & BIRD-LIKE

Hypsilophodontids were once thought to have lived in trees, grasping branches with their feet like giant birds.

The best-known hypsilophodontid is *Hypsilophodon*. When the first fossils of *Hypsilophodon* were found in 1849, scientists thought that they were the bones of a young *Iguanodon*. After more fossils were found, scientists realised this was a completely new dinosaur. Other hypsilophodontid fossils have been found all over the world. The biggest hypsilophodontid was *Tenontosaurus* from North America.

Hypsilophodontids were small and agile dinosaurs, with long, slender four-toed back legs. They had short front legs and stubby five-fingered hands. Their long fingers and toes led scientists to think that hypsilophodonitids might have been good at climbing trees. However, the muscles in their legs indicate that they were probably fast land runners. Hypsilophodontids had powerful jaws and grinding teeth. This helped them to chew tough plant material efficiently.

Hypsilophodon
This dinosaur had strong back legs and a horny beak for snipping off leaves. Hypsilodophodon had four fingers and a little spike on each foot.

WHERE DID THEY LIVE?

Dryosaurus and *Tenontosaurus*
Hypsilophodon

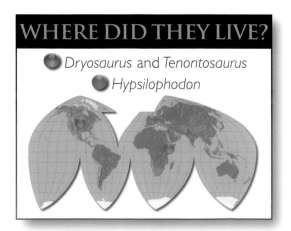

1. Dryosaurus 2. Hypsilophodon   3. Tenontosaurus

Tenontosaurus

A much bigger dinosaur than other hypsilophodontids, Tenontosaurus weighed up to 1 tonne. It had a powerful tail, which might have been used to strike attacking predators, such as Deinonychus.

FACTFILE: HYPSILOPHODON

Lived: 140 to 120 million years ago

Group: Ornithopoda

Size: 2 m long

Weight: 50 kg

Discovery: 1849, England

Diet: herbivore

Special features: strong legs, beak

Name means: 'high-ridged tooth'

Dryosaurus

Like Hypsilophodon, Dryosaurus had a horny beak, but it had no front teeth. With its powerful back legs, this dinosaur was able to wander great distances, and the species spread all over the world.

HOW DO I SAY THAT?

DRYOSAURUS
DRY-OH-SAW-RUS

HYPSILOPHODON
HIP-SIL-OAF-OH-DON

TENONTOSAURUS
TEN-ONT-OH-SAW-RUS

ORNITHOPODS

Hypsilophodon was one of the most successful small ornithopods. Hypsilophodonitids were similar to iguanodontids such as *Iguandon*. However, hypsilophodonitids had smaller, more sharply pointed teeth and a horny beak. They also had few teeth at the front of their jaws and sometimes even no teeth at all. Many of today's plant-eating animals do not have teeth at the front of their mouths. Sheep, for example, snip off grass by pressing their tongue against a bony plates in the roof of their mouths.

DINO DICTIONARY

- **Femur:** the thigh bone
- **Carnivore:** a meat-eating animal

Hypsilophodon

THE ORNITHOPODS:

- *Dryosaurus*
- *Heterodontosaurus*
- *Hypsilophodon*
- *Lesothosaurus*
- *Scutellosaurus*
- *Tenontosaurus*

Running machine

Hypsilophodon *was a typical fast-running dinosaur. Its skeleton shows that with its backbone level, and its legs pumping away below,* Hypsilophodon *may have been able to run at speed for long distances. The weight of its body in front and the tail behind were equal, so* Hypsilophodon *balanced like a seesaw over its back legs.*

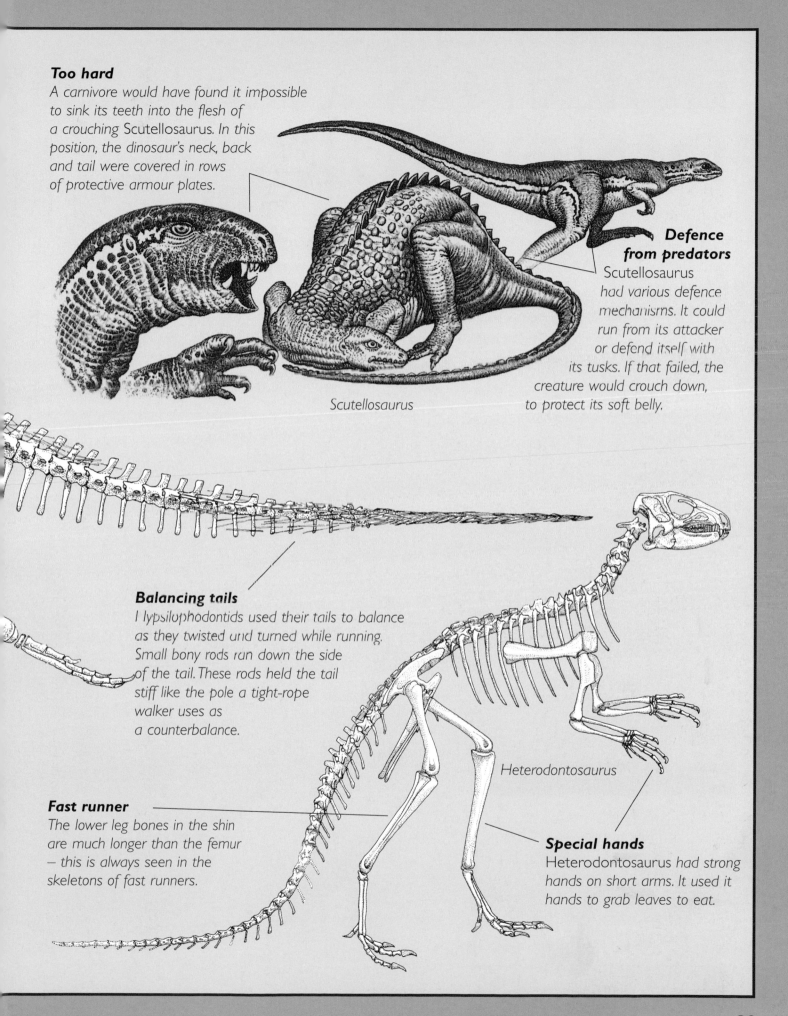

Too hard
A carnivore would have found it impossible to sink its teeth into the flesh of a crouching *Scutellosaurus*. In this position, the dinosaur's neck, back and tail were covered in rows of protective armour plates.

Defence from predators
Scutellosaurus had various defence mechanisms. It could run from its attacker or defend itself with its tusks. If that failed, the creature would crouch down, to protect its soft belly.

Scutellosaurus

Balancing tails
Hypsilophodontids used their tails to balance as they twisted and turned while running. Small bony rods ran down the side of the tail. These rods held the tail stiff like the pole a tight-rope walker uses as a counterbalance.

Fast runner
The lower leg bones in the shin are much longer than the femur — this is always seen in the skeletons of fast runners.

Heterodontosaurus

Special hands
Heterodontosaurus had strong hands on short arms. It used it hands to grab leaves to eat.

HORNLESS DINOSAURS

Early ceratopsians were small, two-legged dinosaurs unlike their giant relatives. All ceratopsians lived in a similar way.

Most of the horn-faced dinosaurs, like *Triceratops* and *Styracosaurus*, were large, four-legged, tank-like animals with huge heads, neck frills and sharp beaks. But the first ceratopsian, *Psittacosaurus*, was human-sized and stood upright on its back legs. Unlike the later ceratopsians, *Psittacosaurus* had no horns. Neither did it sport a big, bony neck frill. Its long legs and powerful grasping hands were similar to those found in ornithopods such as *Hypsilophodon*. So what made it a ceratopsian? The clue is in the shape of its mouth – it was curved like a parrot's beak.

Skeleton

Psittacosaurus *was a slender, two-legged dinosaur, like most ornithopods. However, the sturdy front legs may have been used for walking. The hooked beak suggests that* Psittacosaurus *ate tough plant food, perhaps even tree branches.*

WHERE DID THEY LIVE?

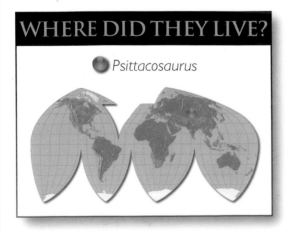

Psittacosaurus

Psittacosaurus

FACTFILE: PSITTACOSAURUS

- Lived: 100 to 90 million years ago
- Group: Ceratopsia
- Size: 1.8 m long
- Weight: 50 kg
- Discovery: 1922, Mongolia
- Diet: herbivore
- Special features: parrot-like beak, strong hands
- Name means: 'parrot reptile'

Plant-eater

Psittacosaurus *fed on leaves and fruit from trees, which it nipped off with its beak and then crushed and sliced at the back of its mouth.*

Little dinosaurs

Baby Psittacosaurus *skeletons were tiny – about the same size as a pigeon. Young dinosaurs had much weaker jaws than adults, so they probably ate tender shoots and berries.*

HOW DO I SAY THAT?

PSITTACOSAURUS
SIT-AK-OH-SAW-RUS

INDEX